Piano • Vocal • Guitar

HOME FOR CHRIS

Amy Grant

ISBN 978-0-7935-2825-7

HAL•LEONARD®

7777 W. BLUEMOUND RD. P.O. BOX 13819 MILWAUKEE, WI 53213

BREATH OF HEAVEN
(MARY'S SONG)

Words and Music by AMY GRANT
and CHRIS EATON

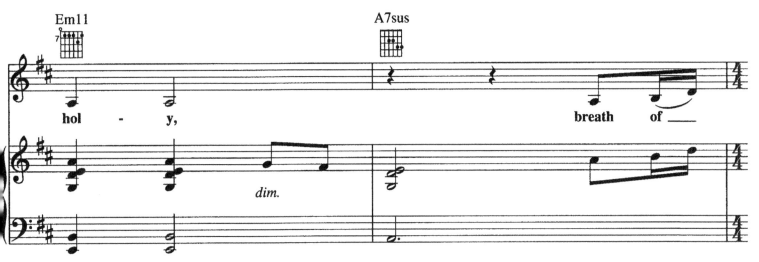

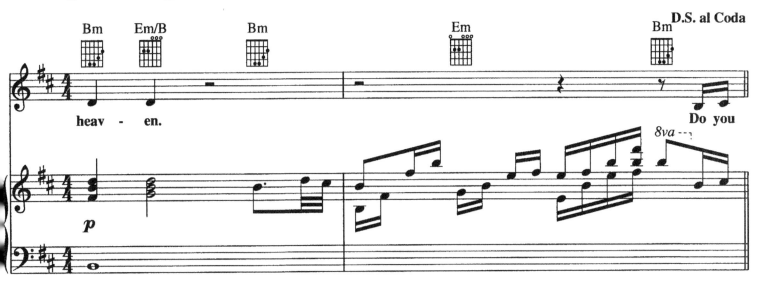

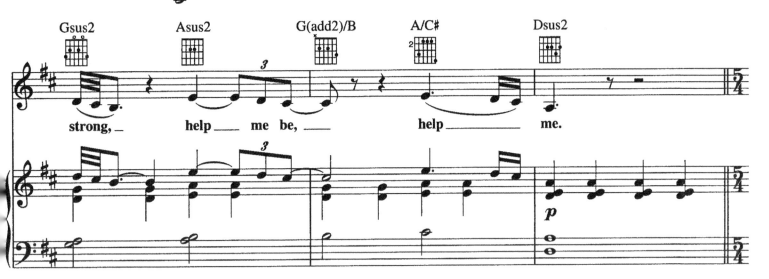

HAVE YOURSELF A MERRY LITTLE CHRISTMAS

Words and Music by RALPH BLANE
and HUGH MARTIN

I'LL BE HOME FOR CHRISTMAS

Words and Music by KIM GANNON
and WALTER KENT

EMMANUEL, GOD WITH US

Words and Music by AMY GRANT,
CHRIS EATON and ROBERT MARSHALL

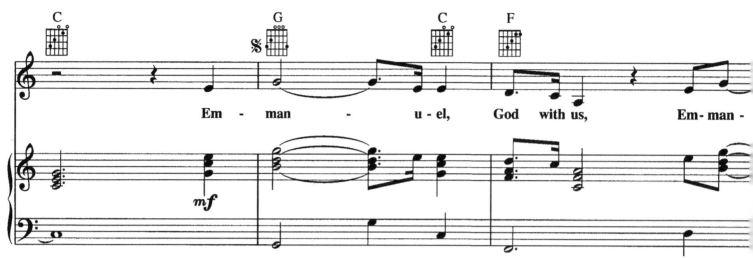

Em - man - u - el, God with us, Em - man -

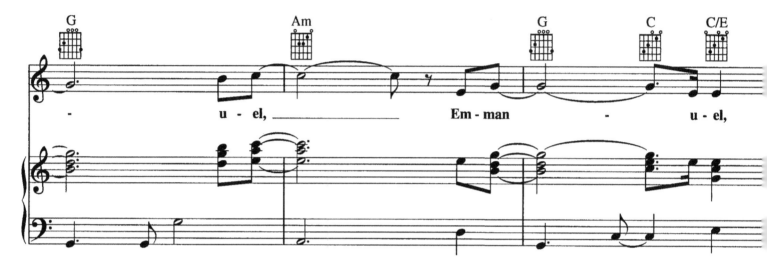

- u - el, _____ Em - man - u - el,

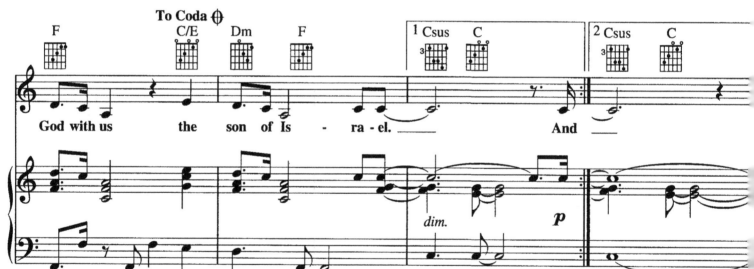

To Coda ⊕

God with us the son of Is - ra - el. _____ And _____

dim.   _p_

And the years, they come, _____ and the years they go, _____ though we

JOY TO THE WORLD/
FOR UNTO US A CHILD IS BORN

FOR UNTO US A CHILD IS BORN
By GEORGE FREDRICK HANDEL
Arranged by RONN HUFF

JOY TO THE WORLD
Music by GEORGE FREDRICK HANDEL
Text by ISAAC WATTS
Arranged by RONN HUFF

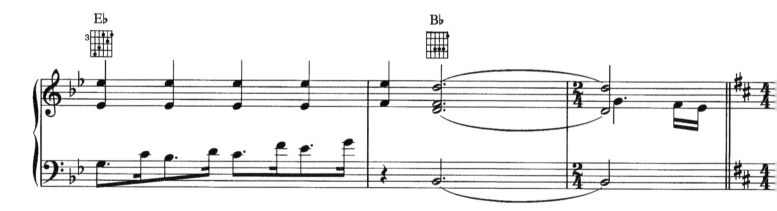

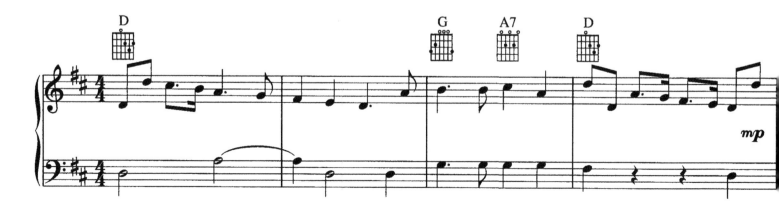

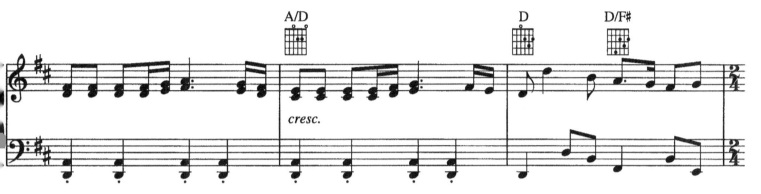

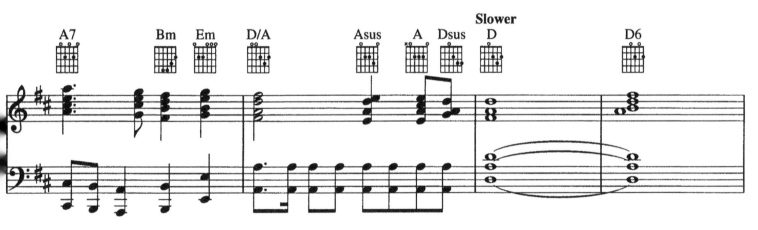

For un-to us a child is born._____ For un-to

JESU, JOY OF MAN'S DESIRING

By JOHANN SEBASTIAN BACH

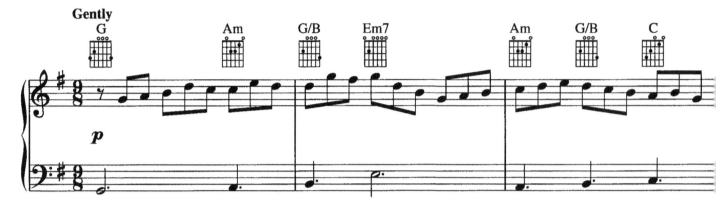

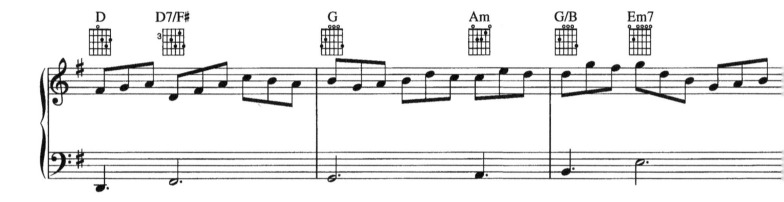

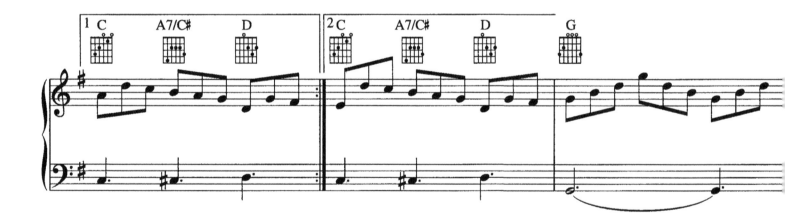

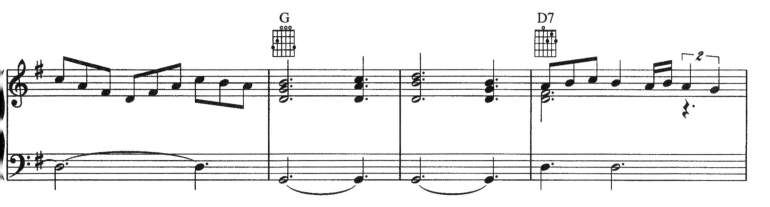

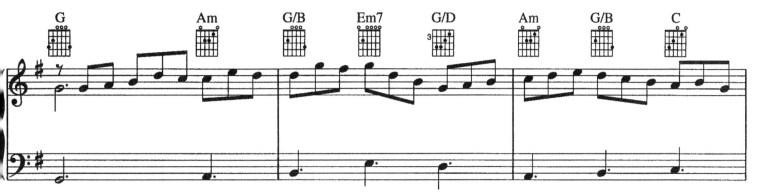

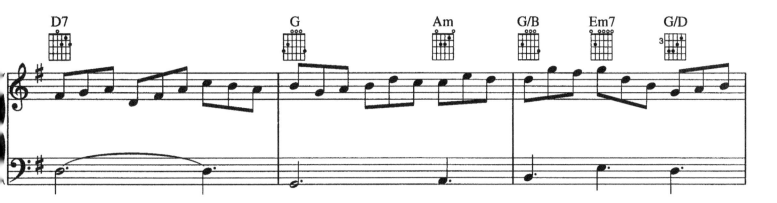

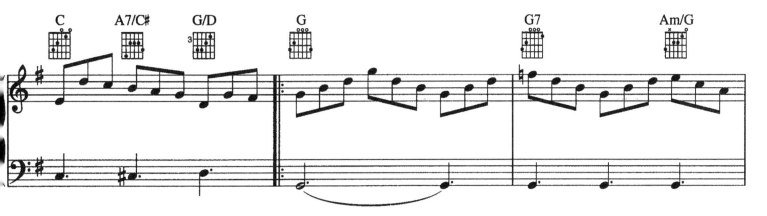

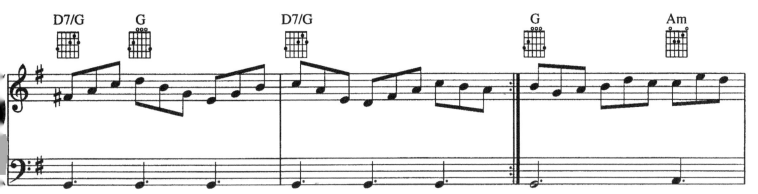

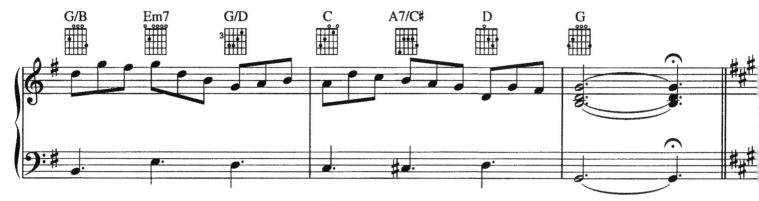

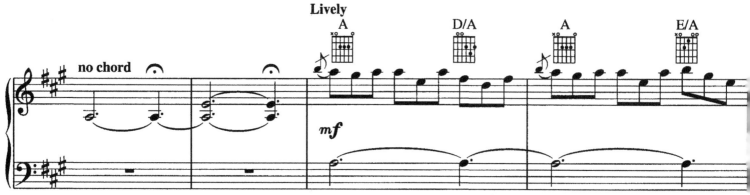

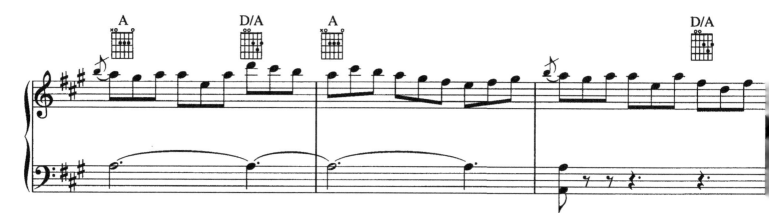

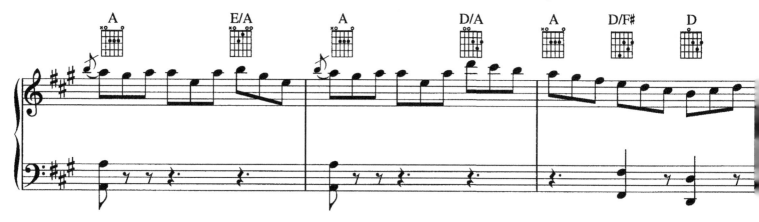

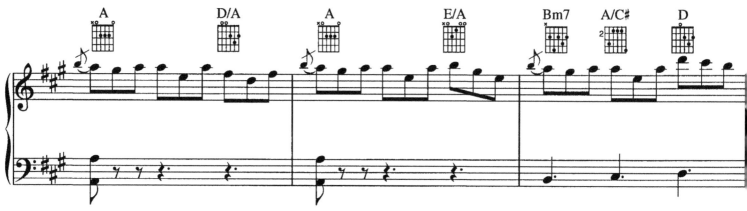

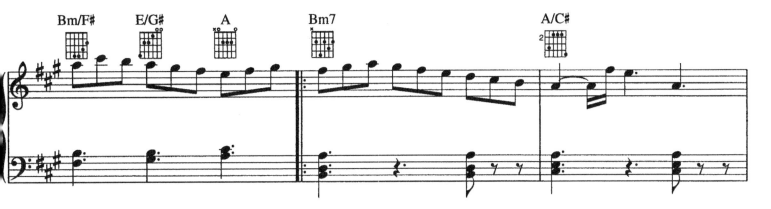

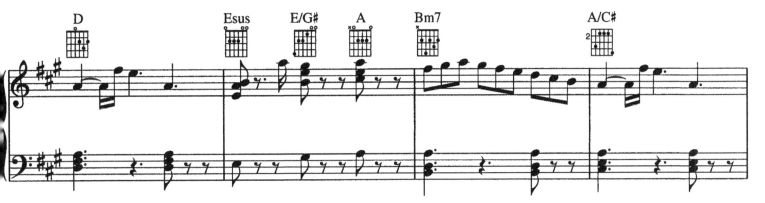

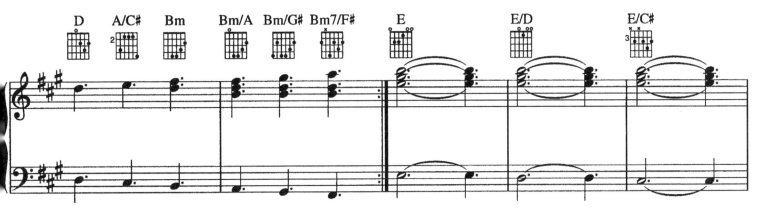

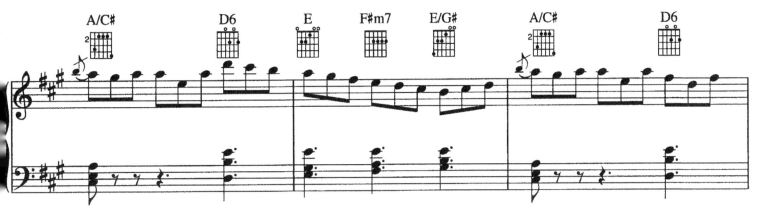

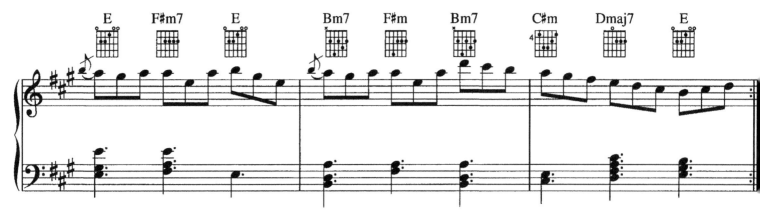

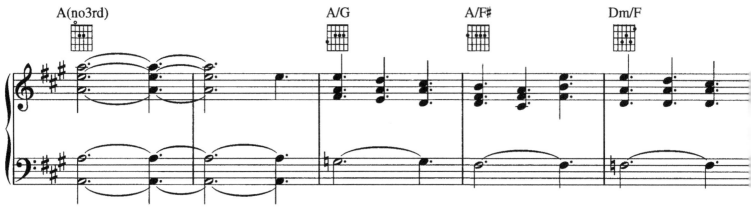

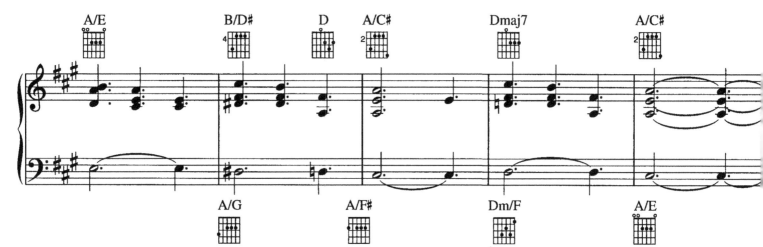

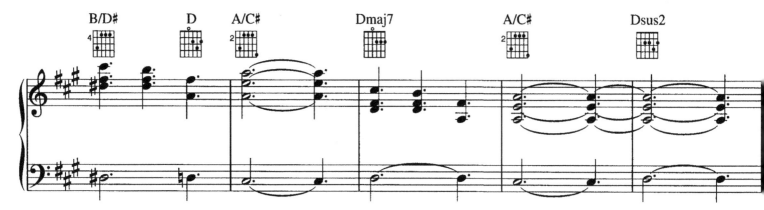

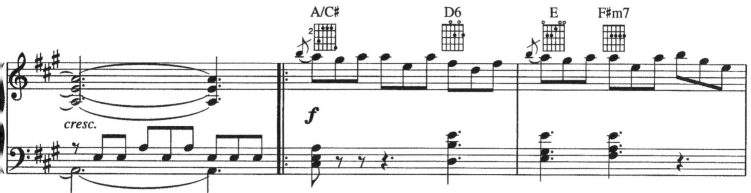

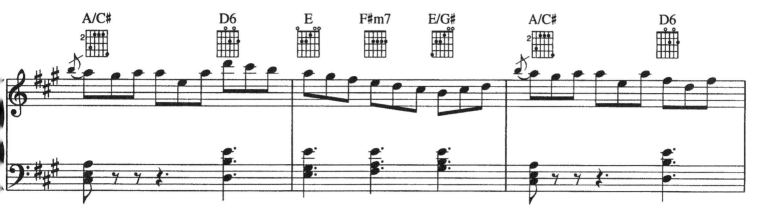

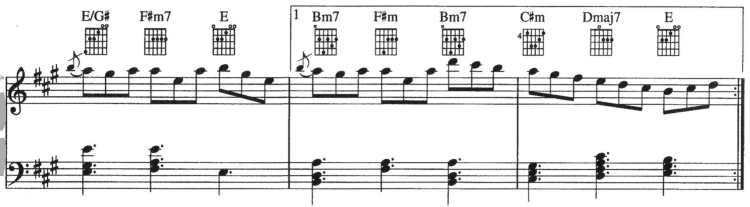

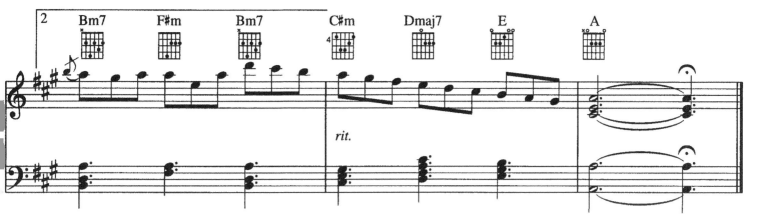

THE MOST WONDERFUL TIME OF THE YEAR

Words and Music by EDDIE POLA
and GEORGE WYLE

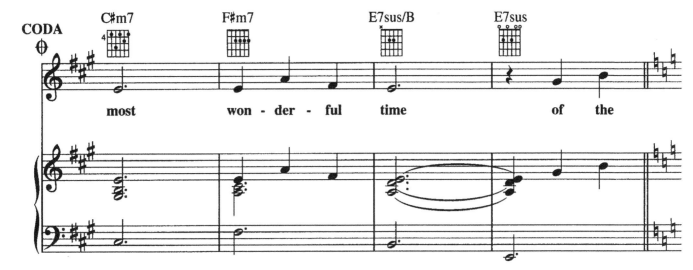

most won - der - ful time of the

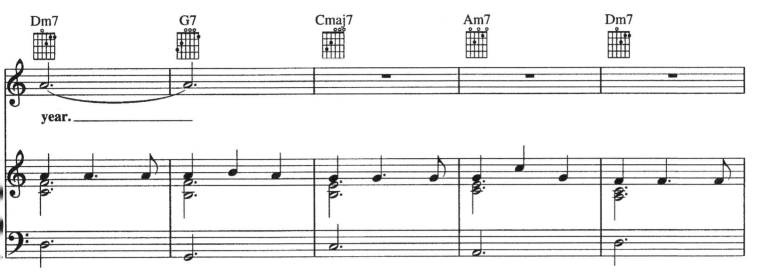

year.

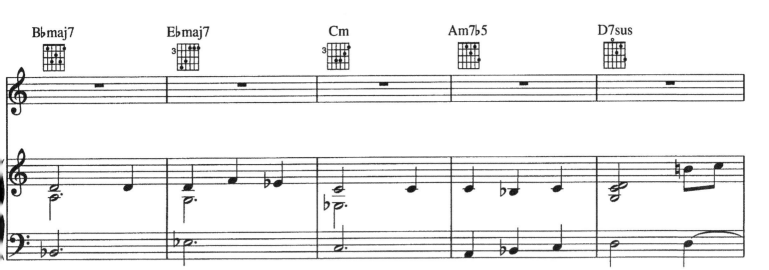

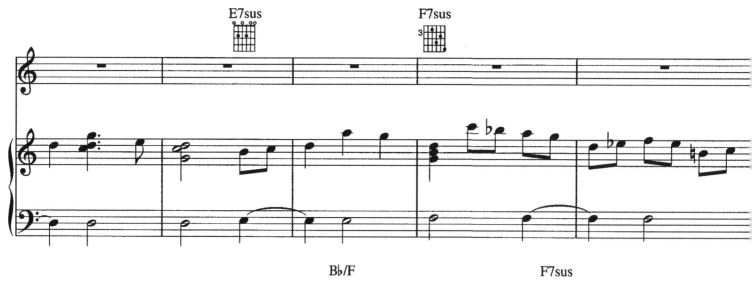

It's the most won-der-ful time of the

year.___ There'll be much mis-tle-toe-ing and

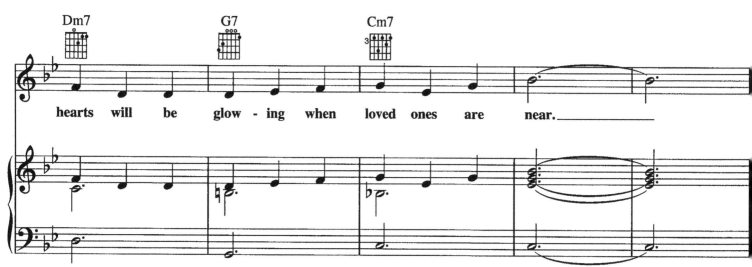

hearts will be glow-ing when loved ones are near.___

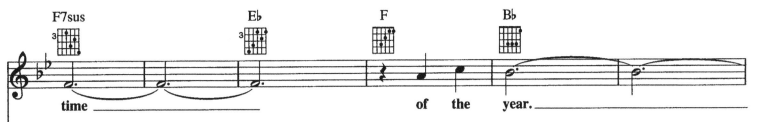

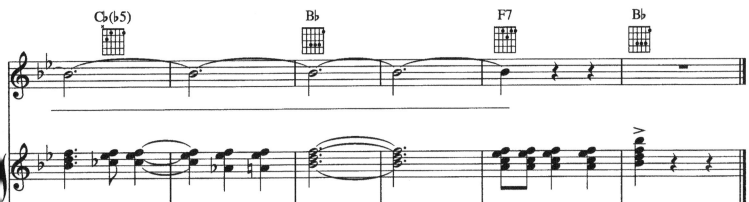

MY GROWN UP CHRISTMAS LIST

Words and Music by DAVID FOSTER
and LINDA THOMPSON JENNER

O COME ALL YE FAITHFUL

Words and Music by
JOHN FRANCIS WADE

come, all ye faith - ful,
Yea Lord, we greet thee,

joy - ful and tri - um - phant.
born this hap - py morn - ing.

O'
O'

come, ye o' come ye to Beth - le -hem.
Je - sus, to thee be all glo - ry giv'n.

THE NIGHT BEFORE CHRISTMAS

Words and Music by
CARLY SIMON

ROCKIN' AROUND THE CHRISTMAS TREE

Music and Lyrics by
JOHNNY MARKS

WINTER WONDERLAND

Words by DICK SMITH
Music by FELIX BERNARD